THE BEST OF

LED-ZEPPELIN

play guitar with....

play guitar with...

THE BEST OF
LED-ZEPPELIN

VOL. 1

WISE PUBLICATIONS
PART OF THE MUSIC SALES GROUP

LONDON / NEW YORK / PARIS / SYDNEY / COPENHAGEN / BERLIN / MADRID / HONG KONG / TOKYO

Published by

Wise Publications
14-15 Berners Street, London W1T 3LJ, UK

Exclusive Distributors:

Music Sales Limited
Distribution Centre, Newmarket Road,
Bury St Edmunds, Suffolk IP33 3YB, UK

Music Sales Pty Limited
20 Resolution Drive,
Caringbah, NSW 2229, Australia

Order No. AM996589
ISBN 978-1-84772-945-3
This book © Copyright 2010 Wise Publications,
a division of Music Sales Limited.

Cover designed by Liz Barrand
Photo research by Jacqui Black

Printed in the EU

www.musicsales.com

RECORDING NOTES

It is simply impossible to actually recreate the recorded performances of Led Zeppelin and the production techniques of Jimmy Page. The intention of these recordings is to aid study of the guitar parts by providing credible backing tracks to play-along with, hopefully capturing the spirit of the original music. Ultimately it is essential to listen to, and try and emulate the original Led Zeppelin tracks to really understand the musical nuance, intensity, and brilliance of those recordings.

CREDITS

Supervisory editors: Brad Tolinski and Jimmy Brown

Project manager and music editor: Tom Farncombe

Additional transcription and editing: Jimmy Brown, Dan Begelman and Jack Allen

Audio recorded and mixed by Jonas Persson

Guitars and guitar transcriptions: Arthur Dick
Bass guitar and bass transcriptions: Paul Townsend
Drums, percussion and drum transcriptions: Noam Lederman

Keyboards and keyboard transcriptions: Paul Honey

Music engraved by Paul Ewers Music Design

With special thanks to Mark Lodge at Hiwatt UK for supplying the Hiwatt 100 Head – an exact replica of Jimmy Page's amp from the Led Zeppelin sessions.

WWW.HIWATT.CO.UK

Also thanks to Chandler guitars (www.chandlerguitars.co.uk).

Arthur Dick

Paul Townsend

Noam Lederman

EQUIPMENT LIST

In addition to the instruments specified below, the following were used for these recordings:

1968 Ludwig drum kit (24" bass drum; 13" rack tom; 16" floor tom; 18" second floor tom)
Ludwig 6.5x14" Supraphonic snare drum; Ludwig 8x14" Coliseum snare drum
Paiste cymbals

1991 'Longhorn' Fender Jazz bass
1978 Fender Precision bass
1962 reissue Fender Jazz bass (strung with flatwound strings)

Ashdown bass amplification

Nord Electro2 modelling keyboard

Miscellaneous Guitar effects:
Fulltone Full-Drive 2
Roger Mayer Treble Booster
Pete Cornish sustain pedal
Celmo Sardine Can compressor
Jim Dunlop Crybaby Wah-wah

1968 Ludwig drum kit

The following notes detail the guitars and amplifiers used on each song, as an indication of how one might try to match the kind of tone Jimmy Page achieved on the original Led Zeppelin recordings. These were chosen according to the information available about the original recording set-ups; however, with other less-controllable factors to consider (studio size, mic type and placement, location, tape machines and recording consoles, for example), choices about the right sound were driven as much by ear as the reported original conditions.

COMMUNICATION BREAKDOWN

The main riff parts for this song were recorded on a 1972 Fender Telecaster through a 10-watt Cornell Romany amplifier and a 1964 Watkins Electronics Westminster 5-watt combo. This combination was intended to capture the tone of Jimmy Page's Supro amps.

The other rhythm parts were recorded on the 1972 Telecaster through a Hiwatt 100 amp; the solo was recorded using a 1969 Telecaster and the Hiwatt.

The organ parts were played on a Nord Electro2, recorded through a 1965 VOX AC30.

DAZED AND CONFUSED

The main parts for this were tracked on a 1959 Gibson Les Paul through the Hiwatt 100; the higher parts with the same guitar through the Cornell combo.

The reverb for the solo sections – played with a violin bow, of course! – is a from a Lexicon PCM91.

WHOLE LOTTA LOVE

The main parts for this were played on a 1952 Goldtop Les Paul reissue through a Hiwatt 100. The panning sliding part in the chorus was recorded as an ascending slide and then reversed and put through an Eventide flanger.

The solo breaks were played on the 1959 Les Paul using the Roger Mayer Treble Booster through a Marshall JCM2000 with a 4x12 cab; this was then overdriven through a Studer A80 tape machine.

Bongos and cymbals were overdubbed for the middle section alongside tape-effected guitar.

HEARTBREAKER

The two guitars for the main sections were a 1969 Telecaster and the 1952 Les Paul, both recorded through the Hiwatt. The solo was recorded using the 1959 Les Paul.

IMMIGRANT SONG

All the parts for this were tracked using the 1952 Les Paul and the Hiwatt; the tremolo parts were played through a Fender 2x12 cab with a Roger Mayer Voodoo Vibe+ vibrato unit.

SINCE I'VE BEEN LOVING YOU

The main parts for this were played on the 1952 Les Paul through a combination of the Hiwatt and Watkins amps.

The solo is on the 1959 Les Paul through the Marshall JCM2000 and the Cornell.

The organ parts were recorded with the Nord Electro2.

John Paul Jones' original bassline was played on the pedals of his Hammond organ; this was recreated here on a Fender Jazz bass with flatwound strings.

BLACK DOG

The rhythm parts for this song were played on the 1959 Les Paul. This was recorded direct using a Universal Audio DI through a Tubetech CL1B valve compressor, overdriving the input on a Manley valve EQ before being fed back into Pro Tools.

The solo was played on a 1969 Telecaster, using the Hiwatt, the Fender 2x12 cab and with rotary speaker effects derived from a Line 6 MM4 modulation pedal.

ROCK AND ROLL

The rhythm guitars on this song were: A 1952 Les Paul, played through the Hiwatt and Cornell, and a 1969 'Black Beauty' Les Paul through the Cornell and the WEM Westminster combo.

The harmony parts were tracked using the 1969 Telecaster through the Hiwatt and Cornell amps; the solo was played on the same guitar, but using the Marshall.

GUITAR TABLATURE EXPLAINED

Guitar music can be notated in three different ways: on a musical stave, in tablature, and in rhythm slashes.

RHYTHM SLASHES: are written above the stave. Strum chords in the rhythm indicated. Round noteheads indicate single notes.

THE MUSICAL STAVE: shows pitches and rhythms and is divided by lines into bars. Pitches are named after the first seven letters of the alphabet.

TABLATURE: graphically represents the guitar fingerboard. Each horizontal line represents a string, and each number represents a fret.

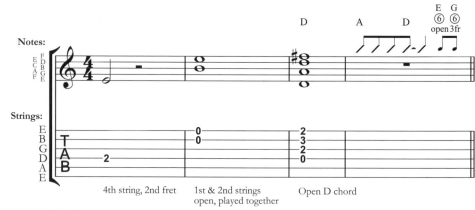

4th string, 2nd fret   1st & 2nd strings open, played together   Open D chord

DEFINITIONS FOR SPECIAL GUITAR NOTATION

SEMI-TONE BEND: Strike the note and bend up a semi-tone (½ step).

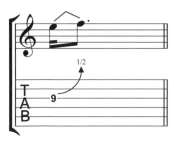

WHOLE-TONE BEND: Strike the note and bend up a whole-tone (full step).

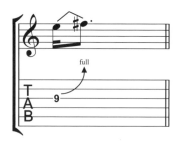

GRACE NOTE BEND: Strike the note and bend as indicated. Play the first note as quickly as possible.

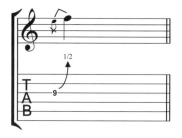

QUARTER-TONE BEND: Strike the note and bend up a ¼ step

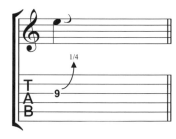

BEND & RELEASE: Strike the note and bend up as indicated, then release back to the original note.

COMPOUND BEND & RELEASE: Strike the note and bend up and down in the rhythm indicated.

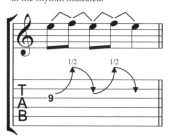

PRE-BEND: Bend the note as indicated, then strike it.

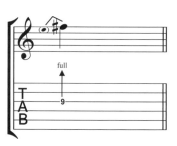

PRE-BEND & RELEASE: Bend the note as indicated. Strike it and release the note back to the original pitch.

HAMMER-ON: Strike the first note with one finger, then sound the second note (on the same string) with another finger by fretting it without picking.

PULL-OFF: Place both fingers on the note to be sounded, strike the first note and without picking, pull the finger off to sound the second note.

LEGATO SLIDE (GLISS): Strike the first note and then slide the same fret-hand finger up or down to the second note. The second note is not struck.

MUFFLED STRINGS: A percussive sound is produced by laying the first hand across the string(s) without depressing, and striking them with the pick hand.

NATURAL HARMONIC: Strike the note while the fret-hand lightly touches the string directly over the fret indicated.

PICK SCRAPE: The edge of the pick is rubbed down (or up) the string, producing a scratchy sound.

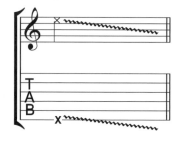

PALM MUTING: The note is partially muted by the pick hand lightly touching the string(s) just before the bridge.

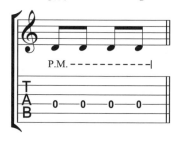

SHIFT SLIDE (GLISS & RESTRIKE): Same as legato slide, except the second note is struck.

TAP HARMONIC: The note is fretted normally and a harmonic is produced by tapping or slapping the fret indicated in brackets (which will be twelve frets higher than the fretted note.)

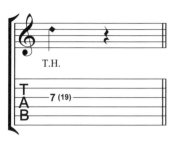

TAPPING: Hammer ('tap') the fret indicated with the pick-hand index or middle finger and pull-off to the note fretted by the fret hand.

PINCH HARMONIC: The note is fretted normally and a harmonic is produced by adding the edge of the thumb or the tip of the index finger of the pick hand to the normal pick attack.

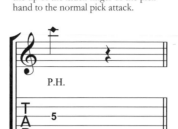

ARTIFICIAL HARMONIC: The note is fretted normally and a harmonic is produced by gently resting the pick hand's index finger directly above the indicated fret (in brackets) while plucking the appropriate string.

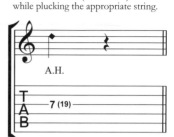

TRILL: Very rapidly alternate between the notes indicated by continuously hammering-on and pulling-off.

RAKE: Drag the pick across the strings with a single motion.

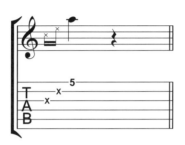

TREMOLO PICKING: The note is picked as rapidly and continously as possible.

ARPEGGIATE: Play the notes of the chord indicated by quickly rolling them from bottom to top.

SWEEP PICKING: Rhythmic downstroke and/or upstroke motion across the strings.

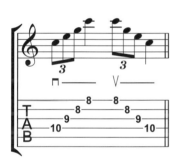

VIBRATO DIVE BAR AND RETURN: The pitch of the note or chord is dropped a specific number of steps (in rhythm) then returned to the original pitch.

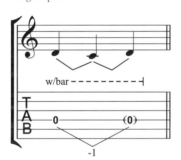

VIBRATO BAR SCOOP: Depress the bar just before striking the note, then quickly release the bar.

VIBRATO BAR DIP: Strike the note and then immediately drop a specific number of steps, then release back to the original pitch.

ADDITIONAL MUSICAL DEFINITIONS

 (accent)   Accentuate note (play it louder)

D.S. al Coda   Go back to the sign (𝄋), then play until the bar marked **To Coda** ⊕ then skip to the section marked ⊕ **Coda**

 (accent)   Accentuate note with greater intensity

D.C. al Fine   Go back to the beginning of the song and play until the bar marked **Fine.**

 (staccato)   Shorten time value of note

tacet   Instrument is silent (drops out).

⊓   Downstroke

V   Upstroke

   Repeat bars between signs

NOTE: Tablature numbers in brackets mean:
1. The note is sustained, but a new articulation (such as hammer-on or slide) begins
2. A note may be fretted but not necessarily played.

When a repeat section has different endings, play the first ending only the first time and the second ending only the second time.

COMMUNICATION BREAKDOWN

Words & Music by
Jimmy Page, Robert Plant, John Paul Jones & John Bonham

Full performance demo: CD 1, track 1
Backing only: CD 2, track 1

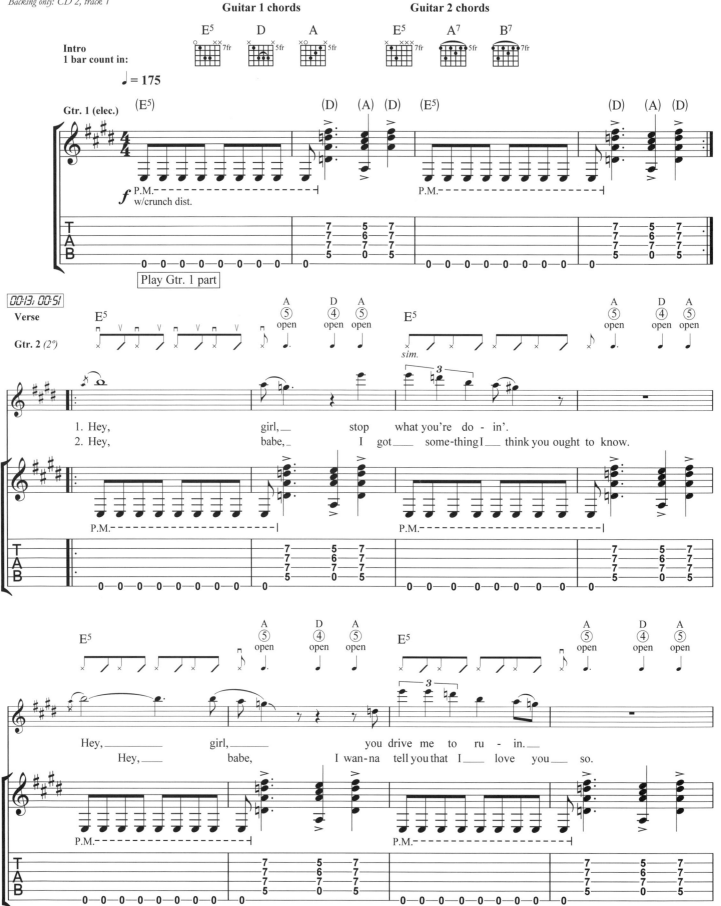

14

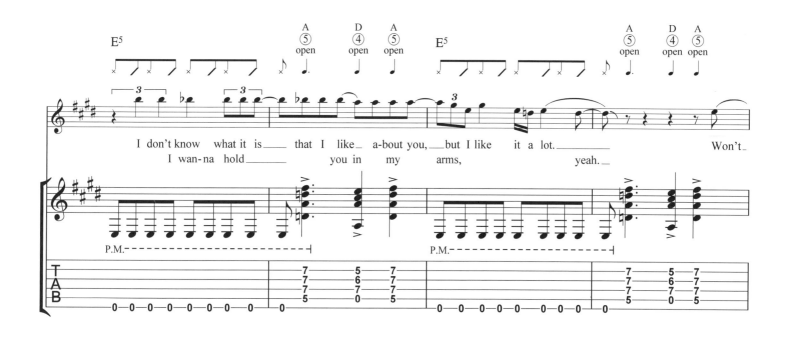

I don't know what it is_____ that I like_ a-bout you,___but I like___ it a lot._____ Won't_
I wan-na hold_____ you in my arms,_____ yeah.__

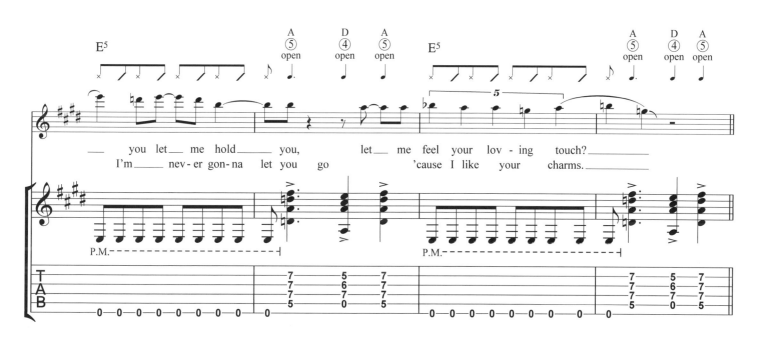

___ you let___ me hold_____ you, let___ me feel your lov-ing touch?_____
I'm_____ nev-er gon-na let you go 'cause I like your charms._____

Gtr. 2 (elec.) A⁷

w/ crunch dist.

Chorus

Com-mu-ni-ca-tion break-down,_ it's al-ways the same._____

Gtr. 1

w/less P.M._____ sim.
Fig. 1 _____

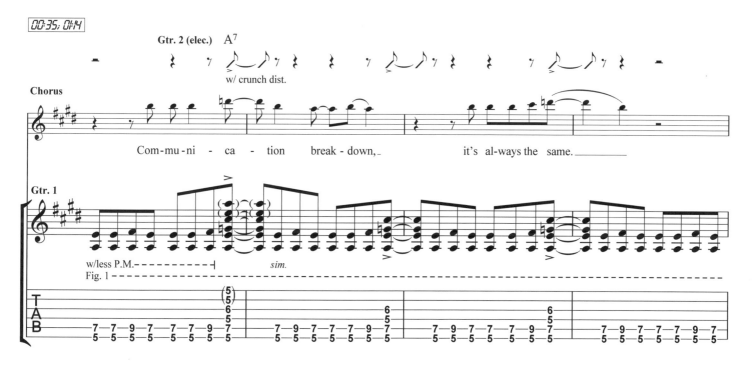

Having a nervous breakdown, drive me insane.

Oh. (Suck!)

Gtr. 1 gradual slide off
Gtr. 2 tacet

Solo

Gtr. 1

Gtr. 2

w/treble dist.

Play Gtr. 2 part

DAZED AND CONFUSED

Words & Music by Jimmy Page

Full performance demo: CD 1, track 2
Backing only: CD 2, track 2

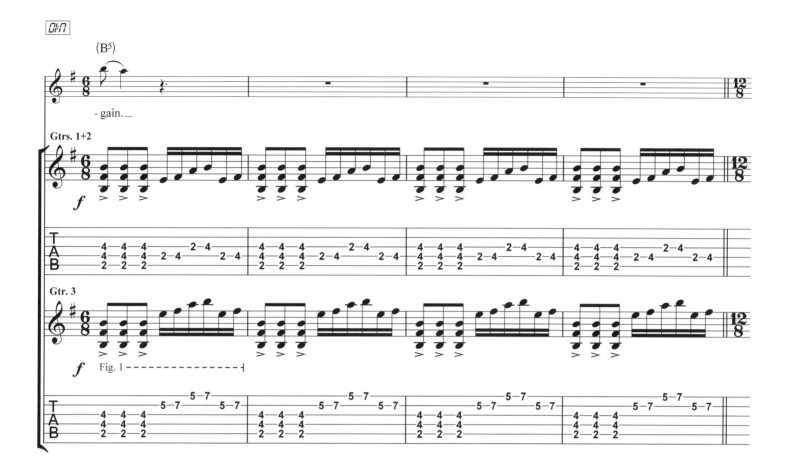

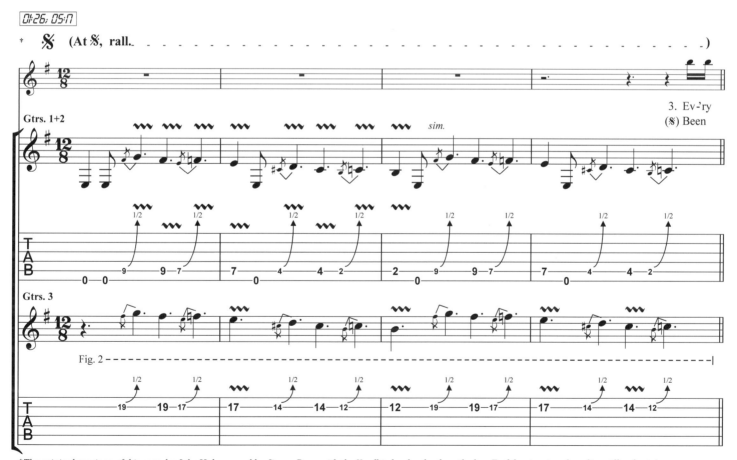

*The original versions of this song by Jake Holmes, and by Jimmy Page with the Yardbirds, clearly place the low E of the signature bass line riff on beat 1 and the high G on beat 2. In the first 2 verses John Bonham chooses to turn the metre around, placing the high G on beat 1. From this point on he clearly turns the metre around again, placing the high G on beat 2 as in the original versions. He remains in this metre for the rest of the song. All subsequent versions of this song follow this exact same pattern of turning the metre around.

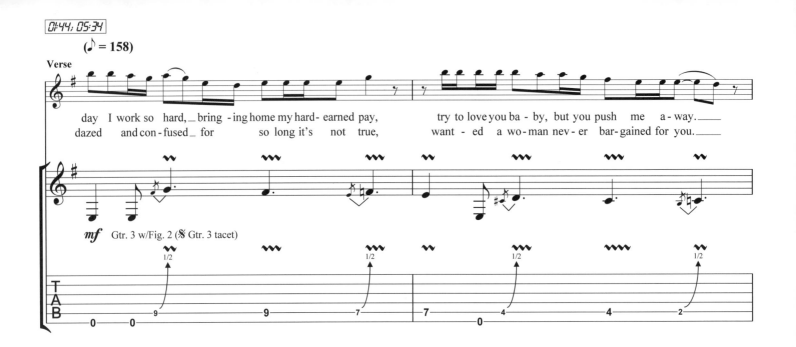

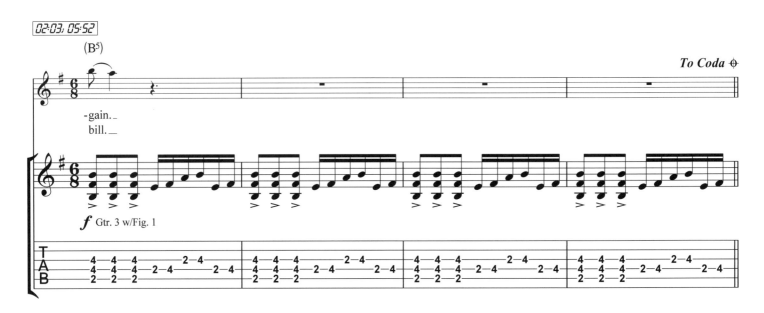

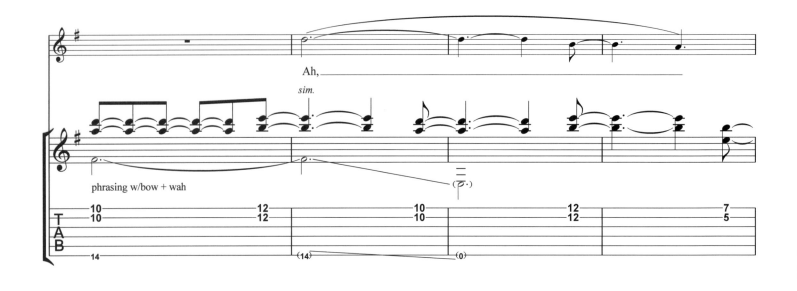

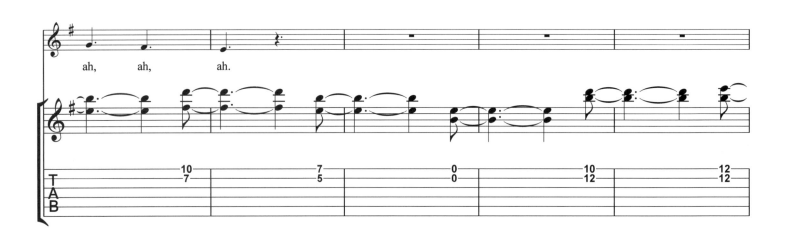

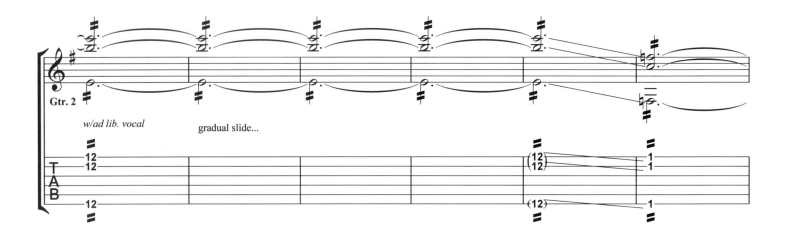

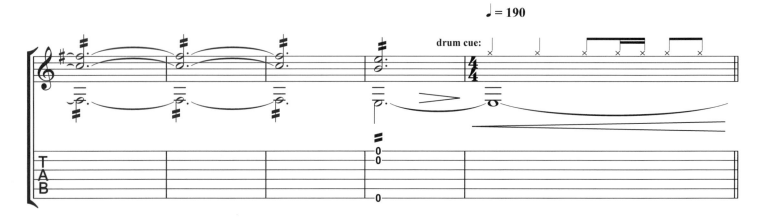

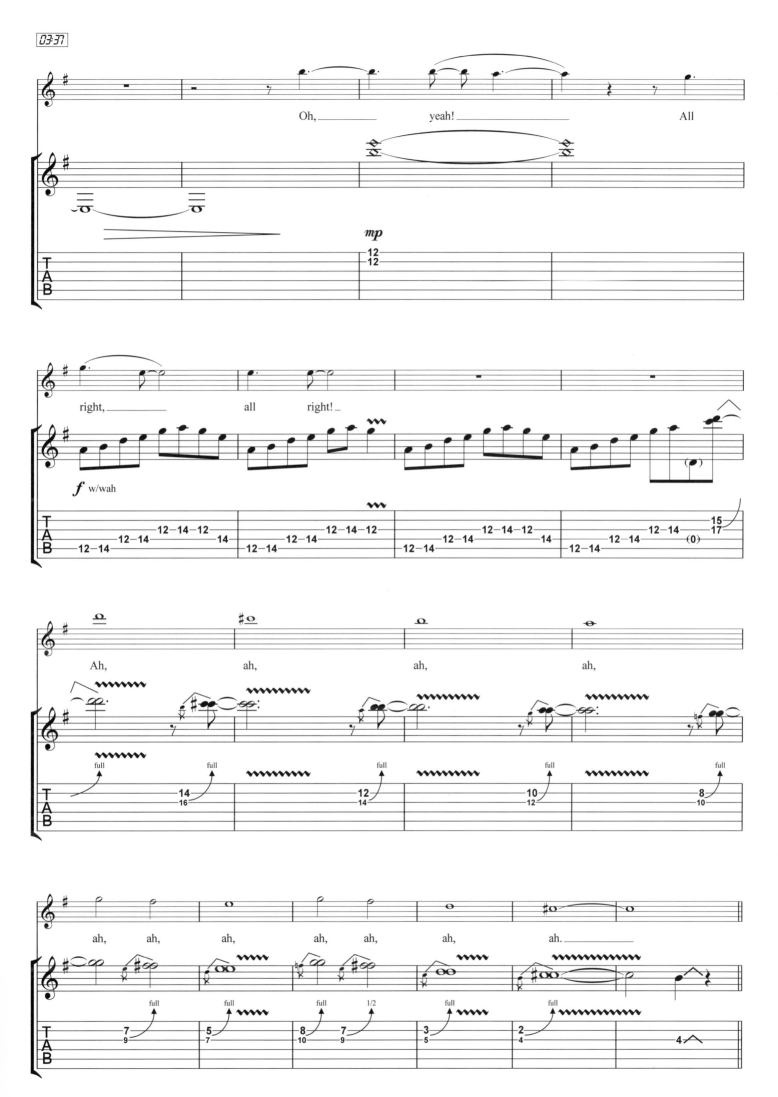

Solo

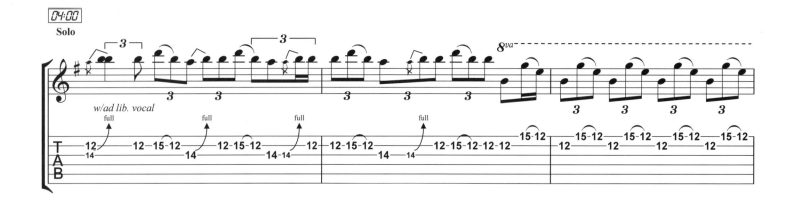

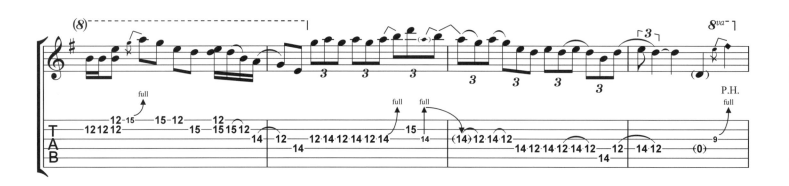

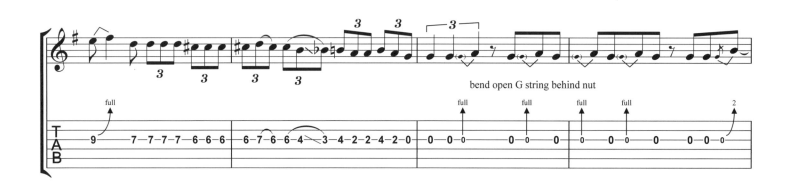

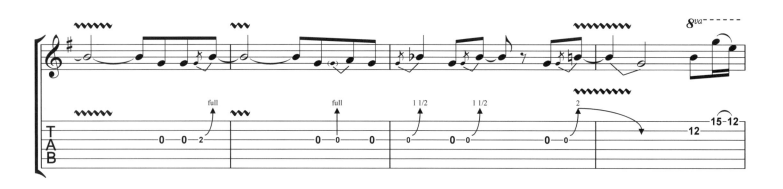

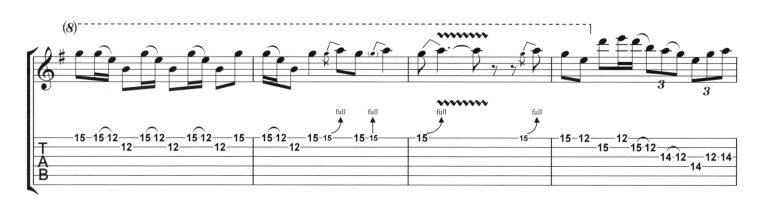

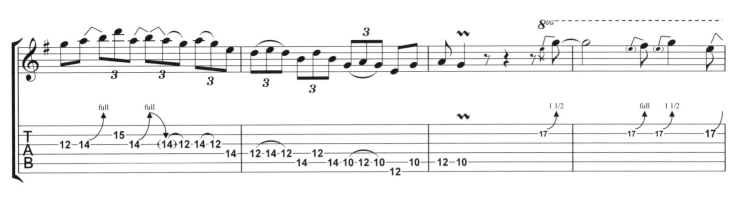

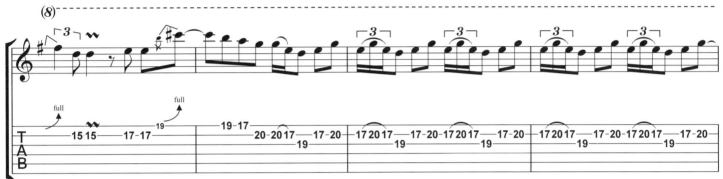

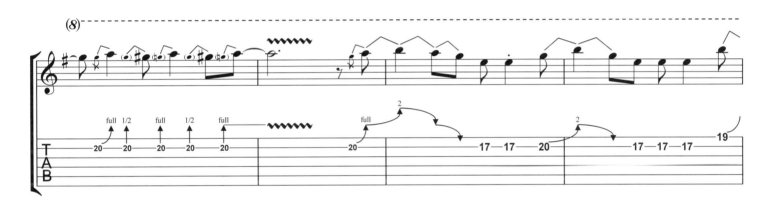

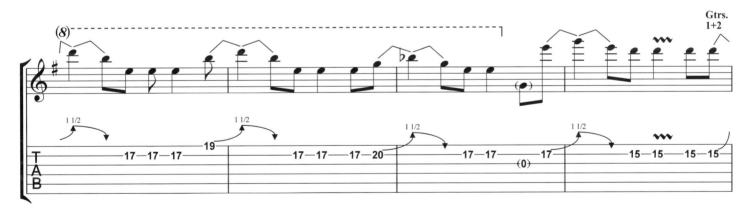

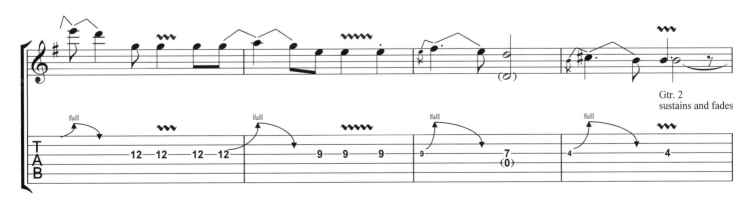

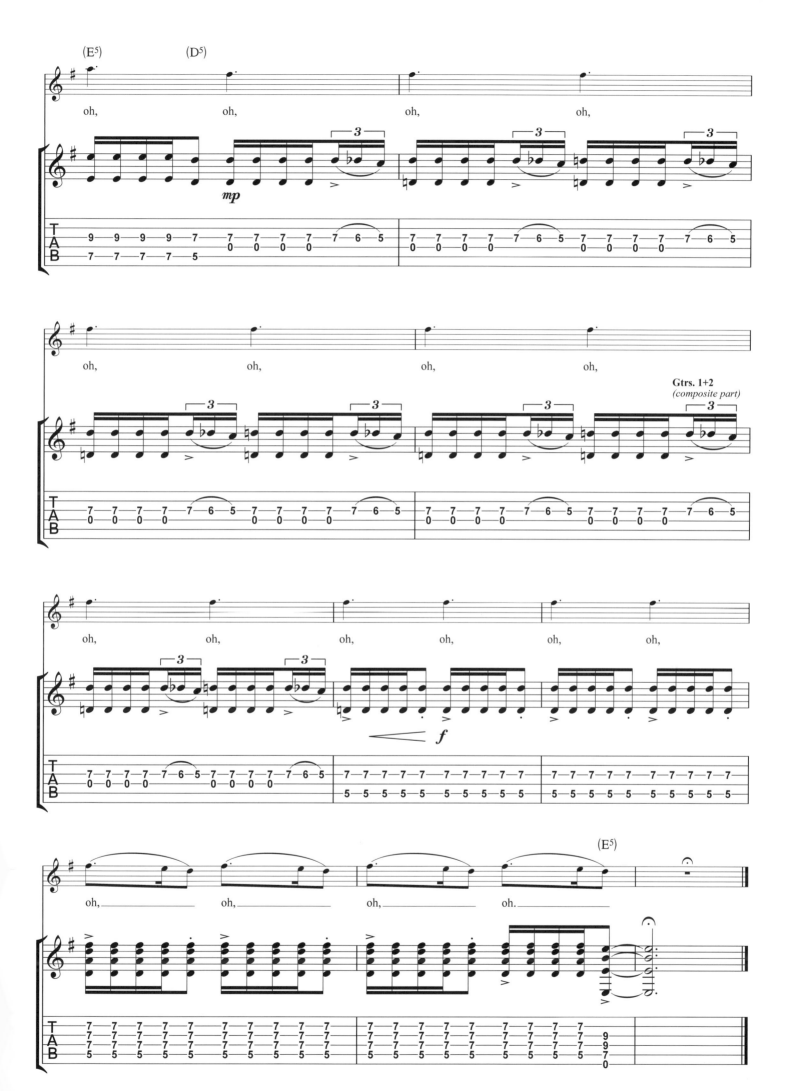

WHOLE LOTTA LOVE

Words & Music by
Jimmy Page, Robert Plant, John Paul Jones & John Bonham

Full performance demo: CD 1, track 3
Backing only: CD 2, track 3

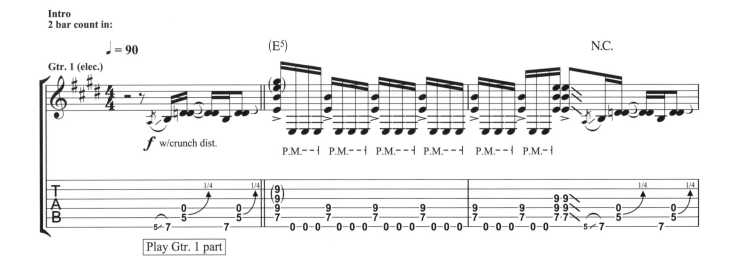

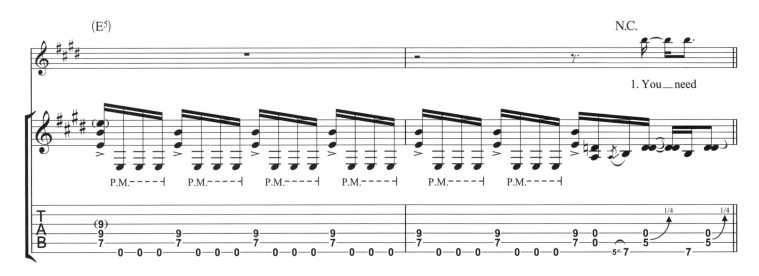

send   you,_____   back   to   school - ing.___
good   times,___   ba - by, ba - by, I've   been   a - yearn - ing,   ah.
All__ the good times___   ba - by__   I've been   mis - us - ing.

Way   down   in - side,   oh, hon-ey you   need__   it.
Ah, way,   way   down   in - side,   oh, hon-ey you   need__   it.
Ah, way,   way   down   in - side,   I'm gon-na give you my__ love.

I'm gon-na give you my__ love,__   I'm gon-na give you my__ love.
I'm gon-na give you my__ love,__   ah,_____   I'm gon-na give you my__ love.   Ah._____
I'm gon-na give you ev-'ry inch of   my__ love._____   I'm gon-na give you my__ love.

You been ___ Wan-na whole lot-ta love. ___

Breakdown

w/*ad lib.* vocal, Theramin, bowed guitar, backwards tape echo fx + percussion

03:04

Gtr. 2 (elec.)

f w/dist. + upper mid-range boost

Gtr. 1

Play Gtr. 2 part

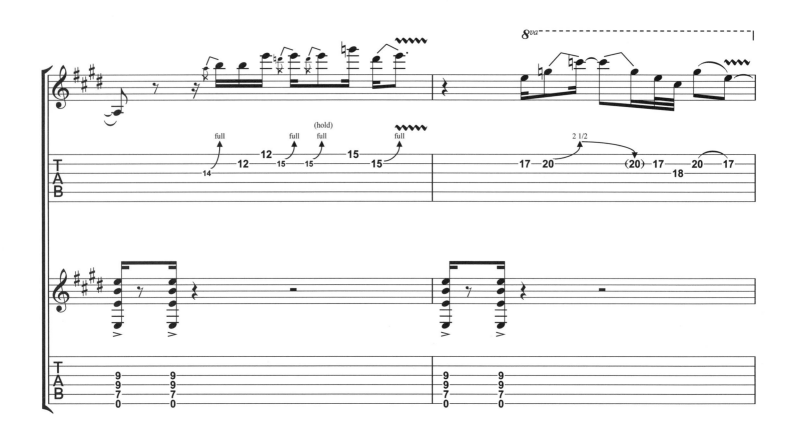

D.S. al Coda

3. You   been

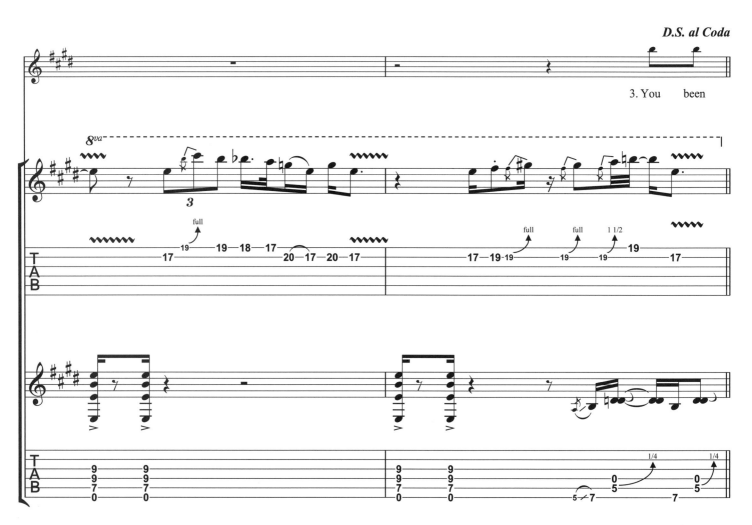

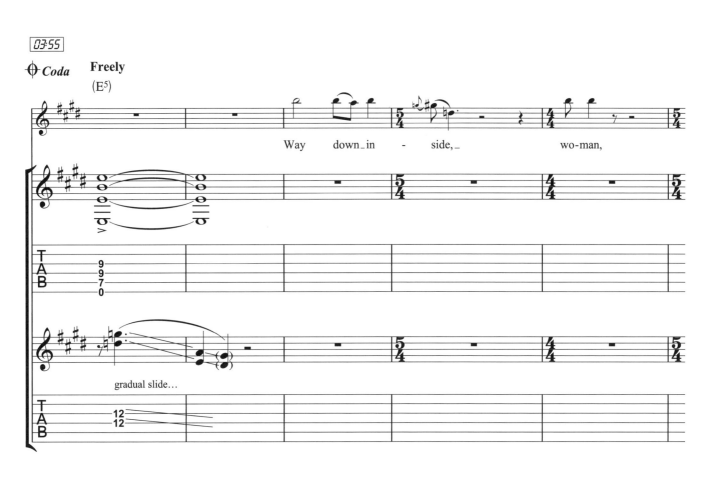

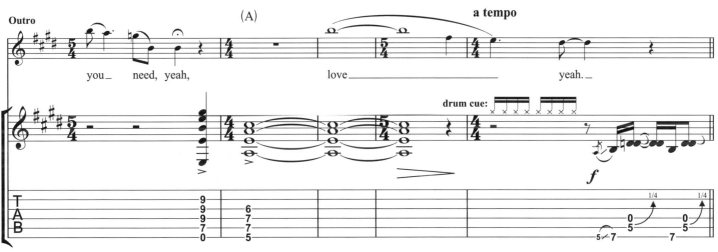

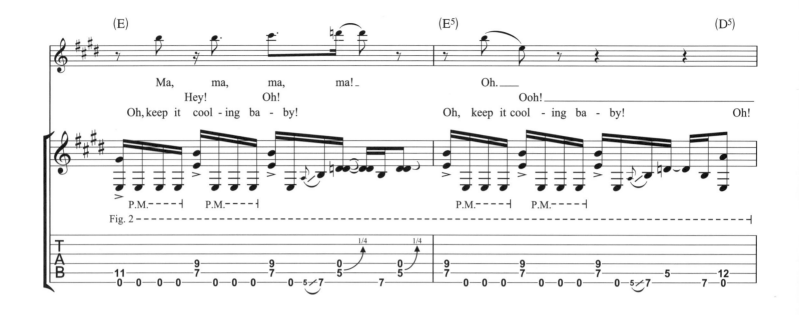

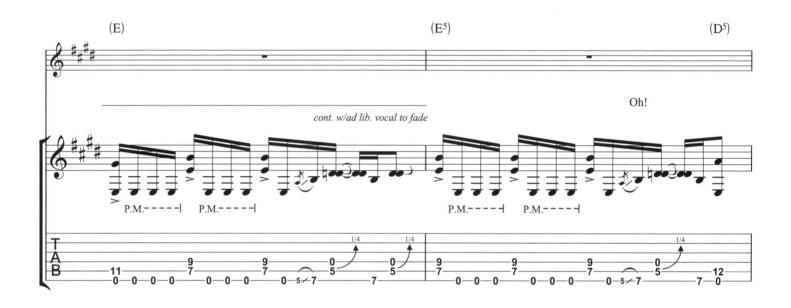

HEARTBREAKER

Words & Music by
Jimmy Page, Robert Plant, John Paul Jones & John Bonham

Full performance demo: CD 1, track 4
Backing only: CD 2, track 4

Intro
1 bar count in:

♩ = 94

Gtrs. 1+2 (elec.)

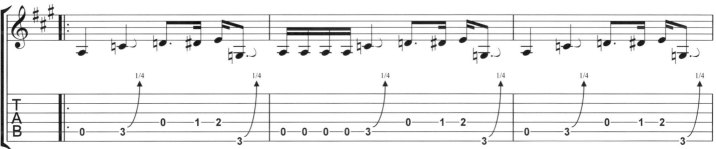

Play Gtr. 1 part

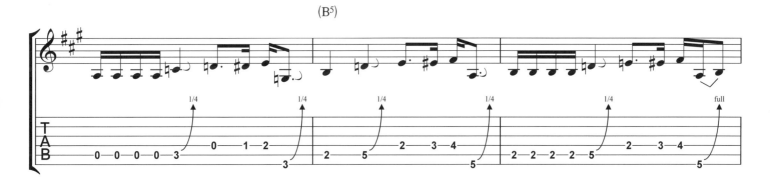

2. Well, it's

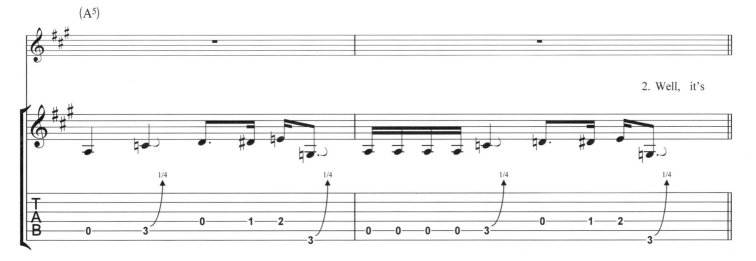

37

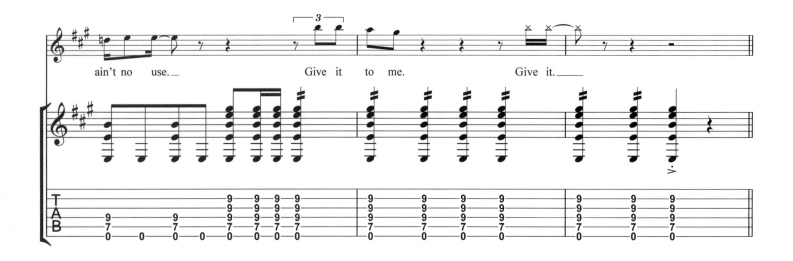

ain't no use.___ Give it to me. Give it.___

02:10
Interlude

Freely

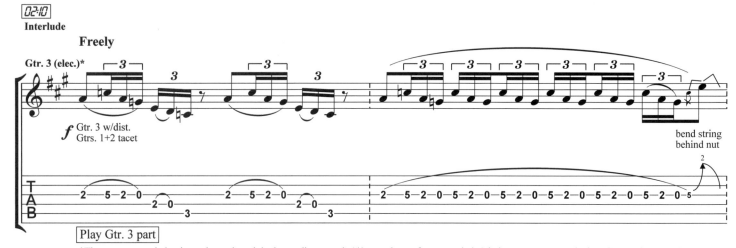

f Gtr. 3 w/dist.
Gtrs. 1+2 tacet

bend string
behind nut

Play Gtr. 3 part

*The unaccompanied guitar solo on the original recording sounds 1/4 tone sharp of concert pitch (pitch returns to normal when Gtrs. 1+2 re-enter).

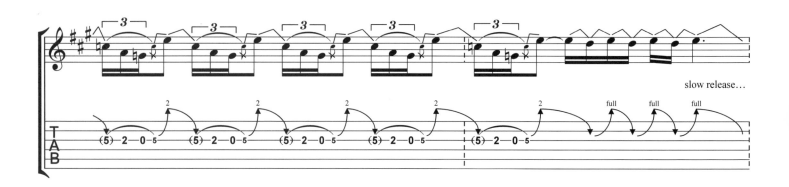

slow release…

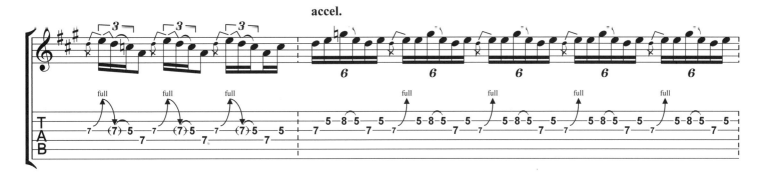
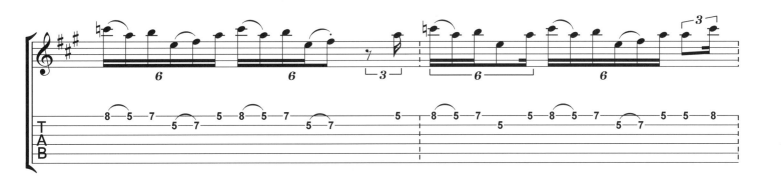

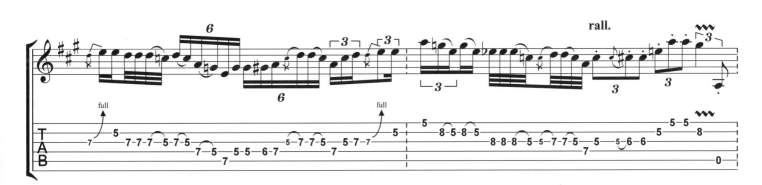

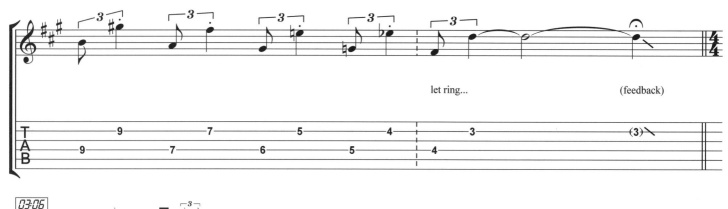

let ring...   (feedback)

Fast ♩ = 211 (♫ = ♪³♪)

Gtr. 2 (elec.)   (A⁷)

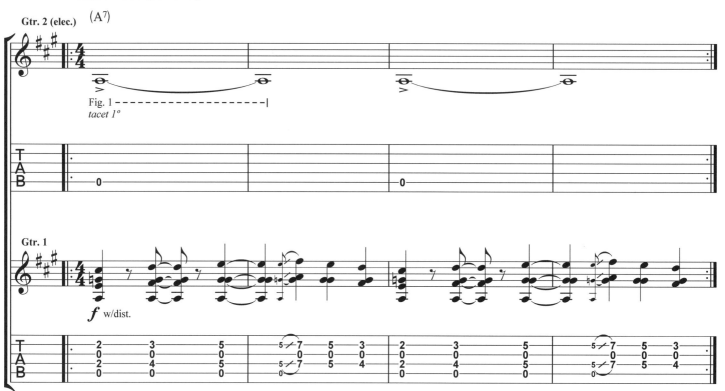

Fig. 1
tacet 1°

Gtr. 1

𝆑 w/dist.

Gtr. 3   (Am⁷)   (D/A)   1.   2.

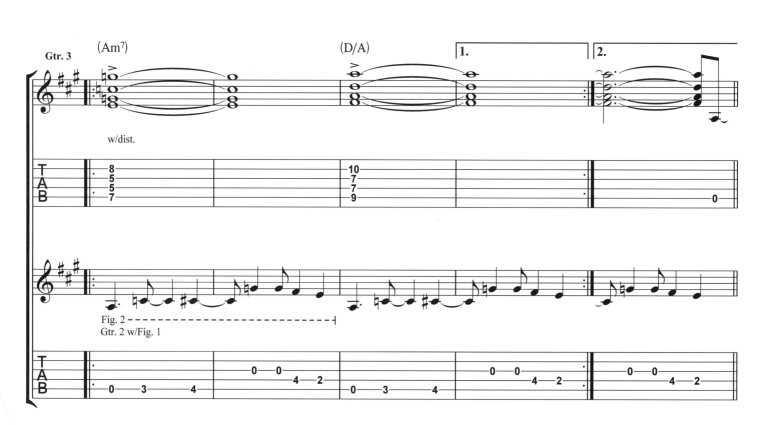

w/dist.

Fig. 2
Gtr. 2 w/Fig. 1

42

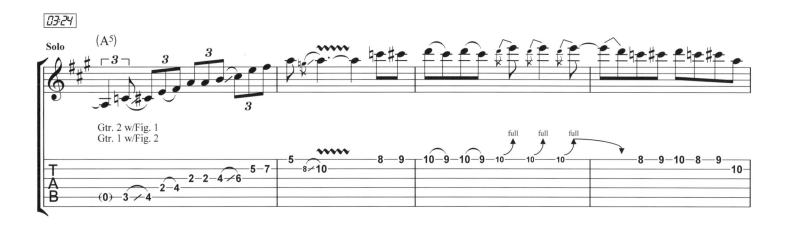

Solo   (A⁵)

Gtr. 2 w/Fig. 1
Gtr. 1 w/Fig. 2

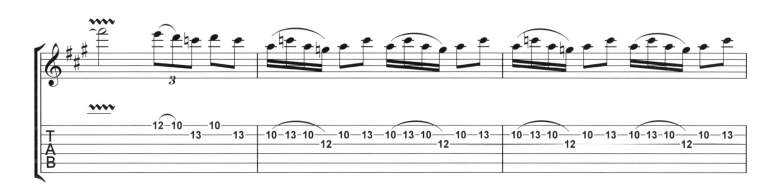

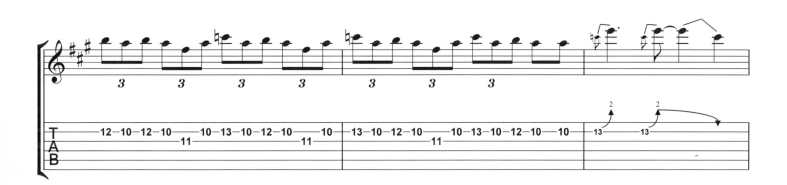

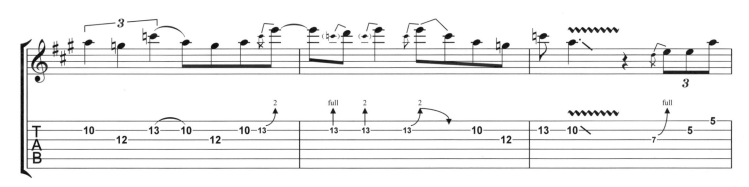

IMMIGRANT SONG

Words & Music by
Jimmy Page & Robert Plant

Full performance demo: CD 1, track 5
Backing only: CD 2, track 5

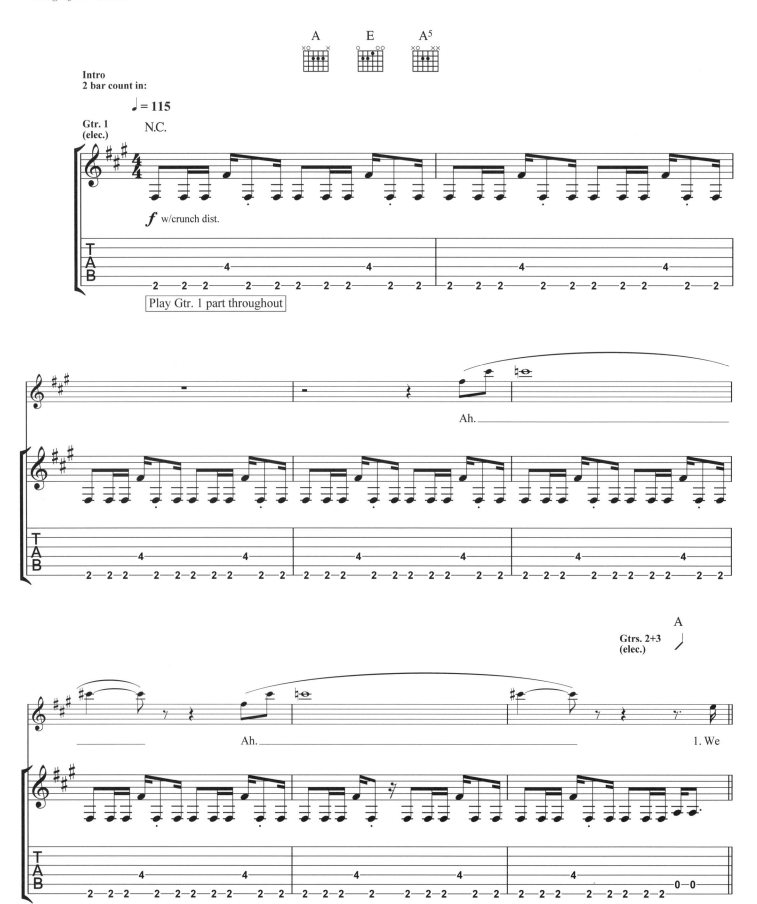

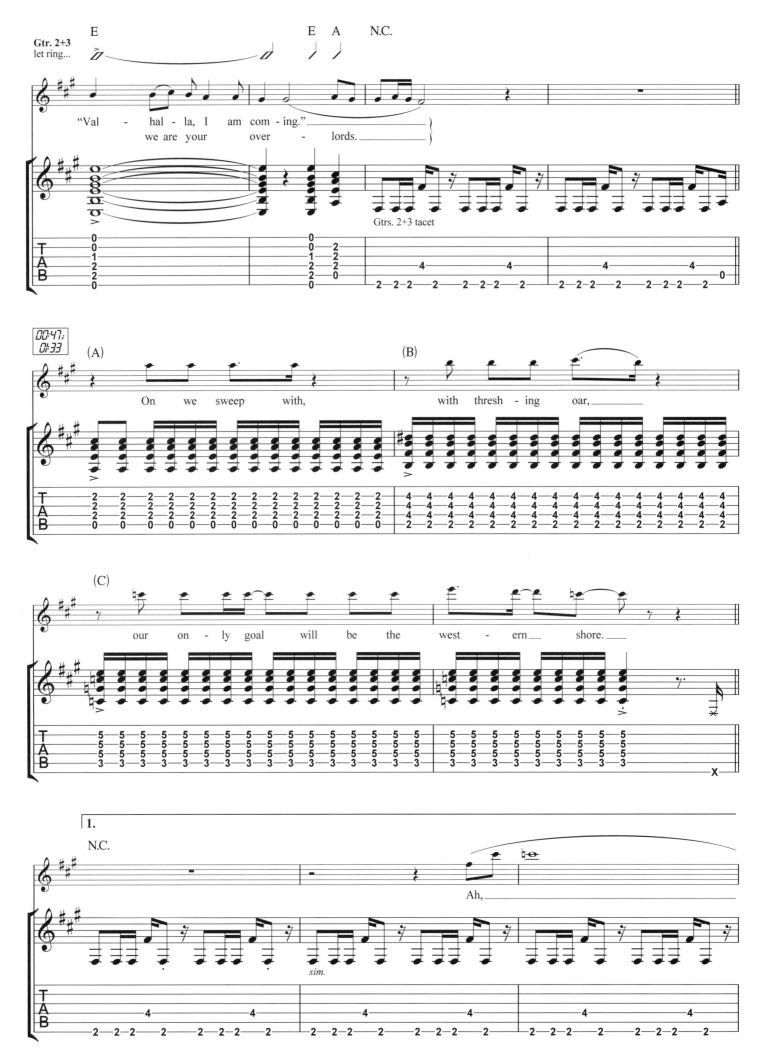

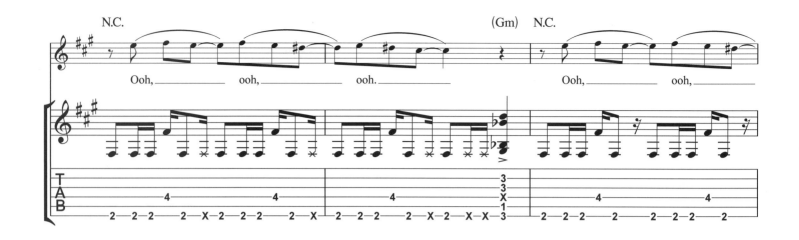

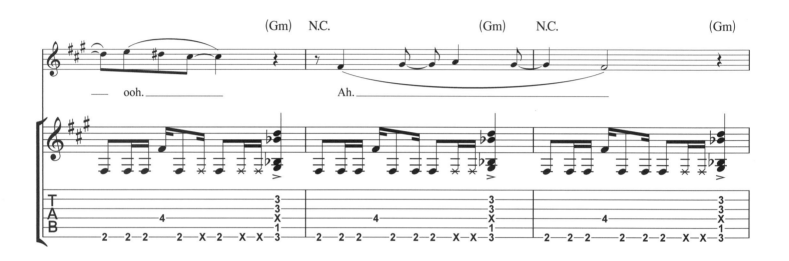

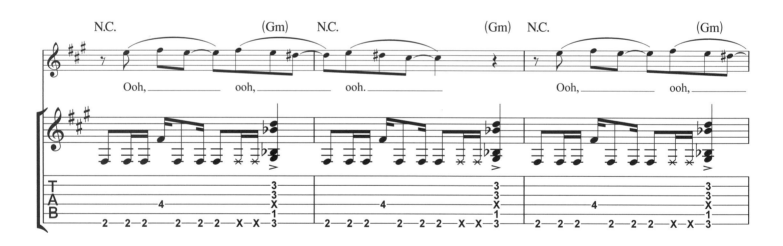

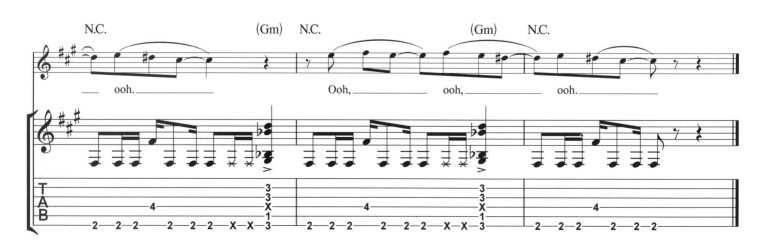

Since I've Been Loving You

Words & Music by
Jimmy Page, Robert Plant & John Paul Jones

Full performance demo: CD 1, track 6
Backing only: CD 2, track 6

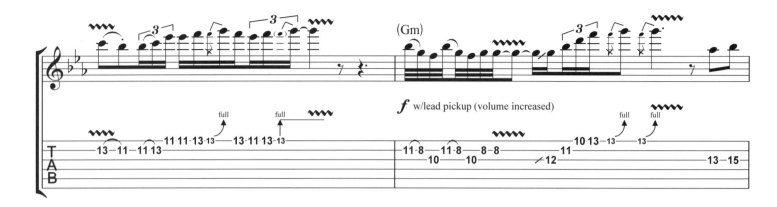

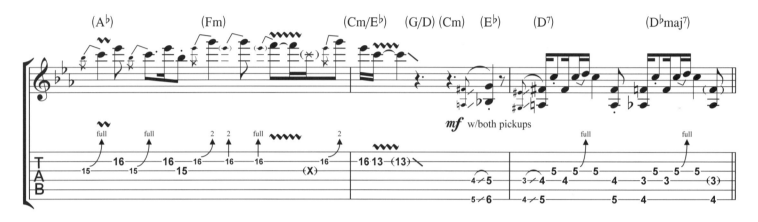

0:18; 02:29

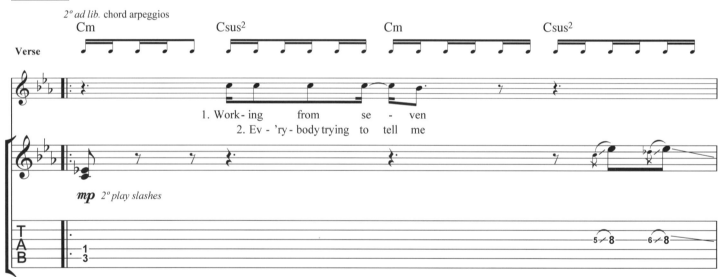

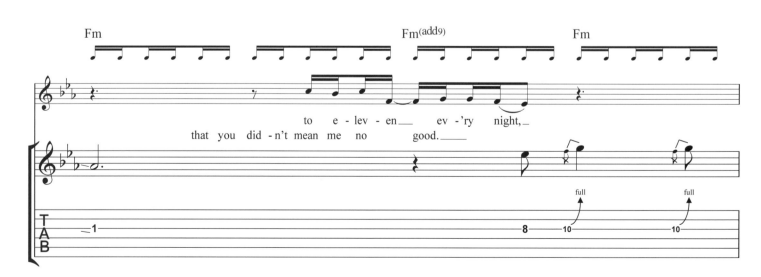

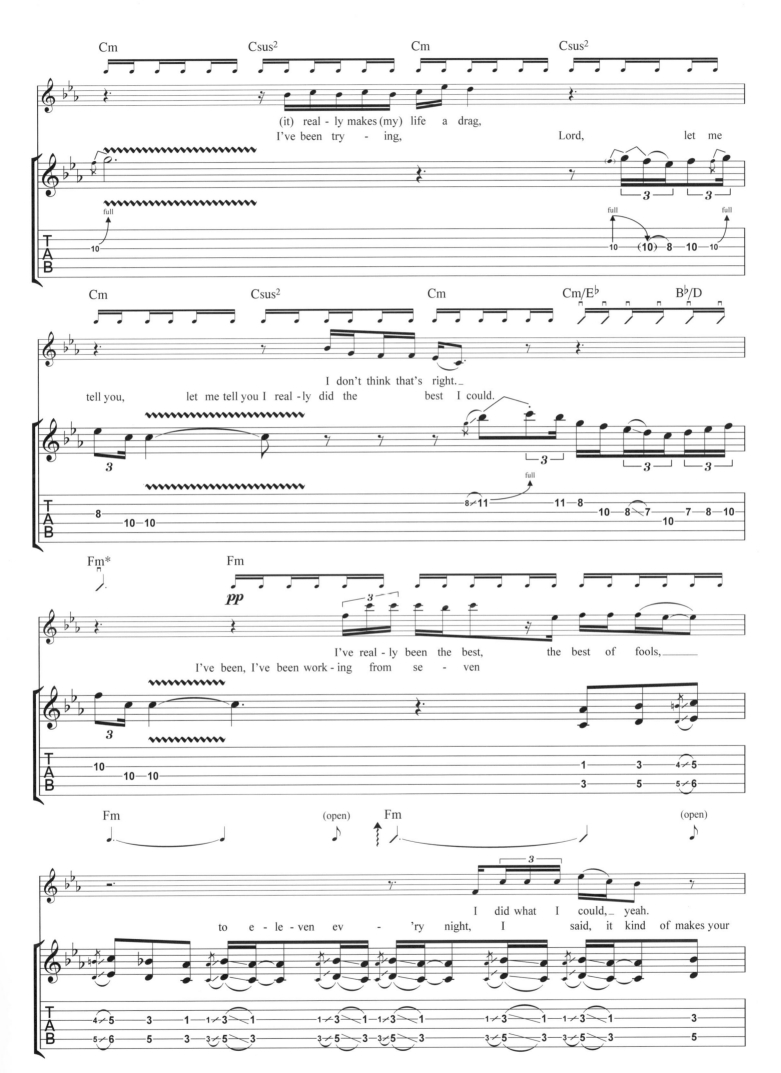

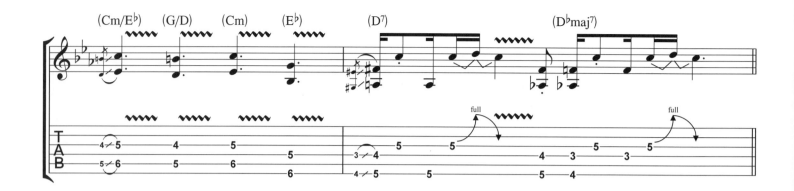

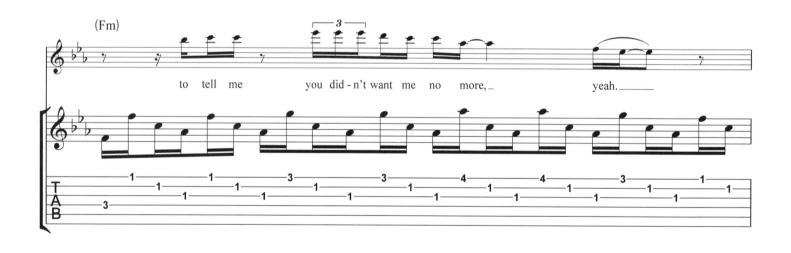

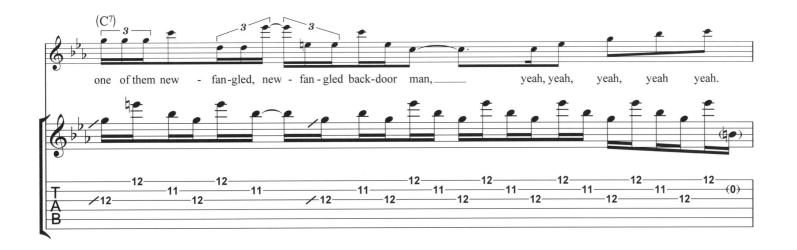

one of them new - fan-gled, new - fan-gled back-door man,_____ yeah, yeah, yeah, yeah yeah.

I've been_work-ing_ from se - ven, se - ven, se - ven to e -

-le - ven ev - 'ry night, it kind - a makes my life a drag,_

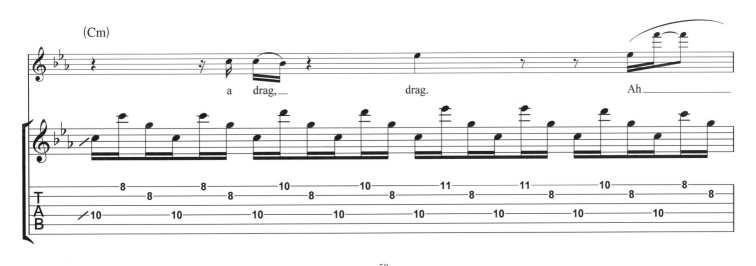

a drag,_ drag. Ah_____

(A♭)

Oh,_____ yeah.

(Fm)

Since I've been lov - ing you, I'm gon - na lose my wor - ried

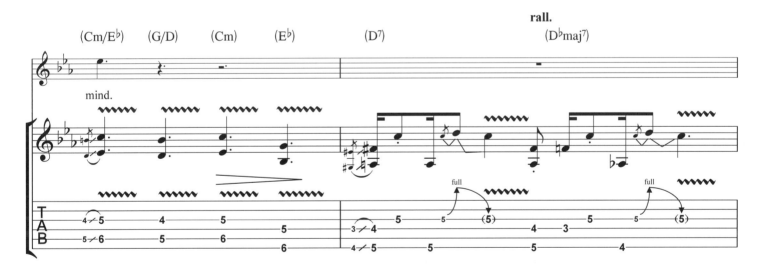

(Cm/E♭)   (G/D)   (Cm)   (E♭)   (D⁷)   **rall.**   (D♭maj⁷)

mind.

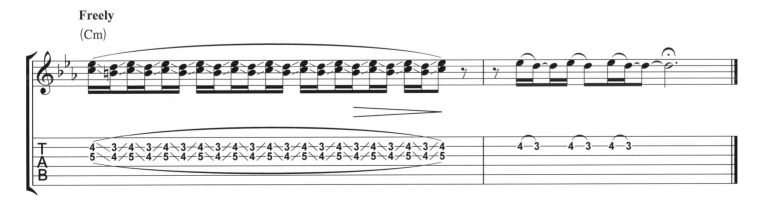

Freely
(Cm)

Black Dog

Words & Music by
Jimmy Page, Robert Plant & John Paul Jones

Full performance demo: CD 1, track 7
Backing only: CD 2, track 7

1. Hey, hey ma-ma, said the way you move, gon-na make you sweat, gon-na make you groove.

2. Ah-ah, child, way you shake that thing, gon-na make you burn, gon-na make you sting.
3. Hey, hey, ba-by when you walk that way,_ watch (your) hon-ey drip,_ can't keep a-way.

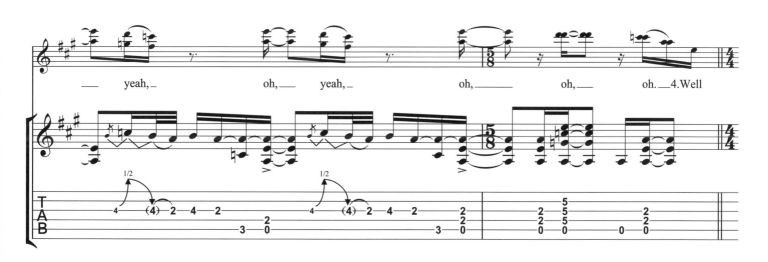

*The metre of this song is somewhat controversial, especially in the **Chorus** and **Solo** sections.*
Previous editions suggest that the kick drum indicates the downbeat, meaning irregular bars at certain points.
However, the drum clicks and cues before these sections would make it seem that the metre actually remains constant, in 4/4;
therefore the snare drum remains on the backbeat throughout. This is reflected in this arrangement.

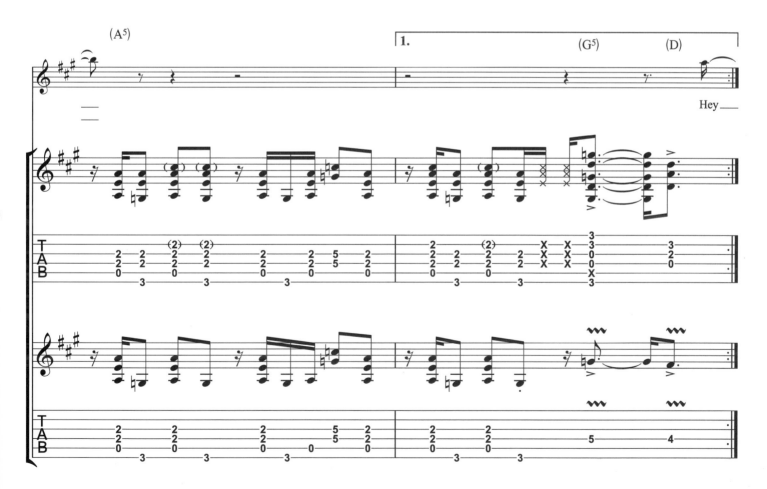

Rock and Roll

Words & Music by
Jimmy Page, Robert Plant, John Paul Jones & John Bonham

Full performance demo: CD 1, track 8
Backing only: CD 2, track 8

71

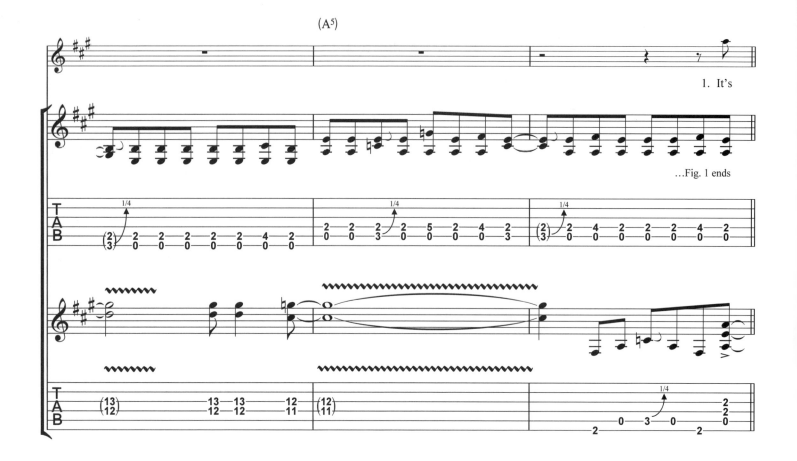

(A5)

1. It's

...Fig. 1 ends

00:28; 01:00; 02:24

𝄋
Verse

(A5)

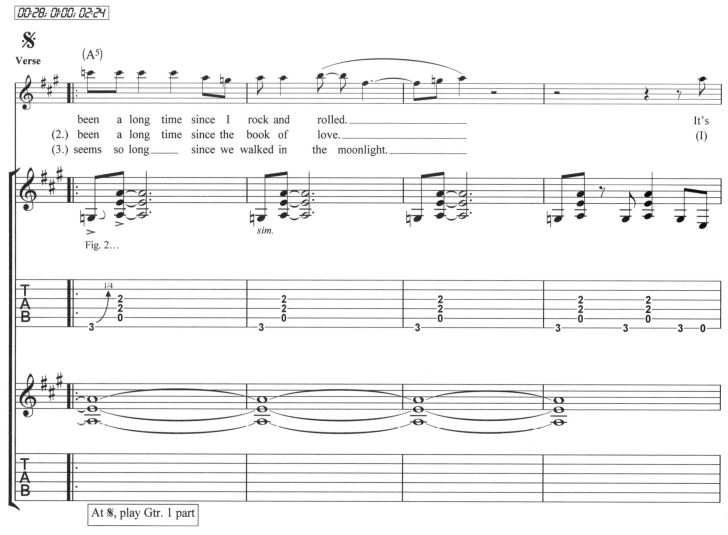

	been	a long	time	since I	rock and	rolled._____	It's
(2.)	been	a long	time	since the	book of	love._____	(I)
(3.)	seems	so long____	since we	walked in	the moonlight._____	

Fig. 2...

sim.

At 𝄋, play Gtr. 1 part

72

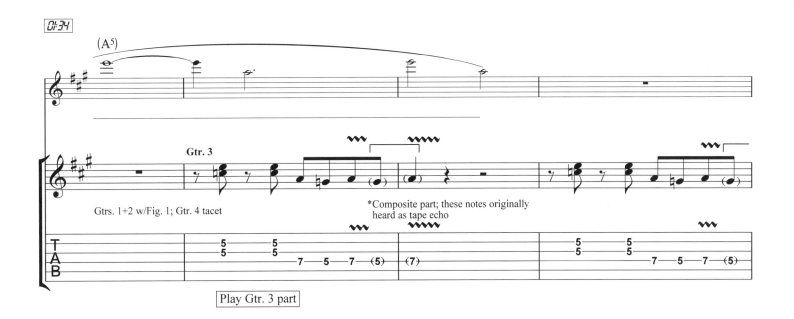

Play Gtr. 3 part

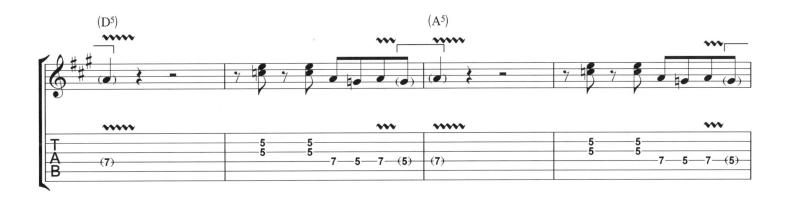

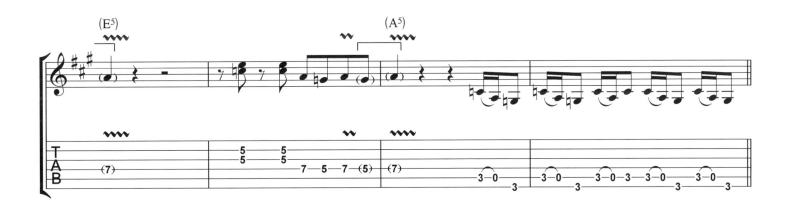

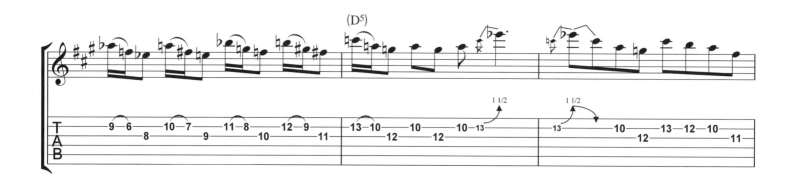

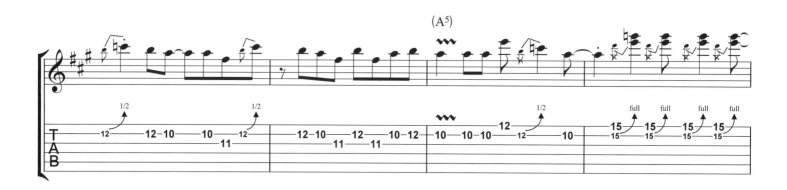

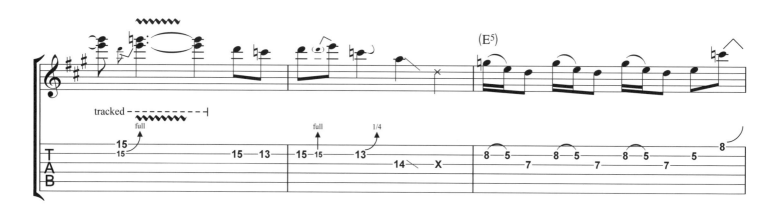

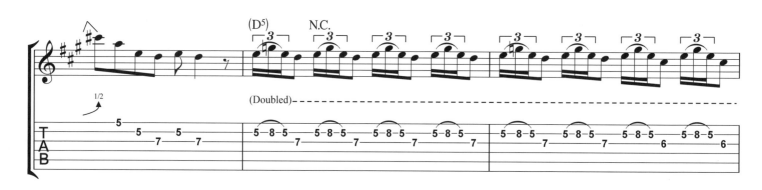

*Regularly played live variant, not performed on original recording

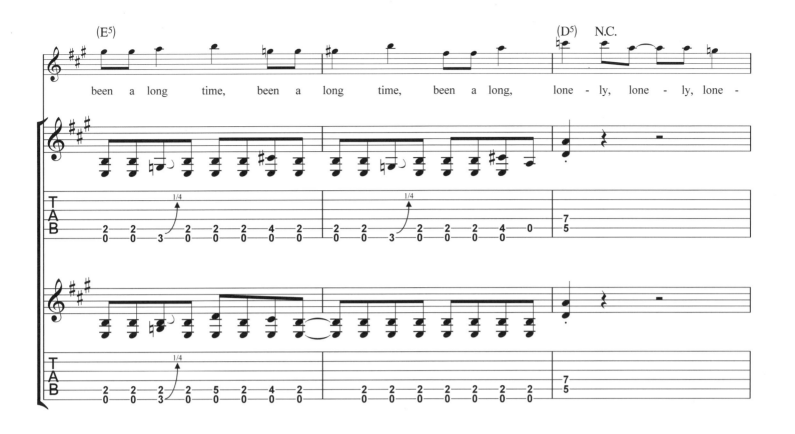

been a long time, been a long time, been a long, lone - ly, lone - ly, lone -

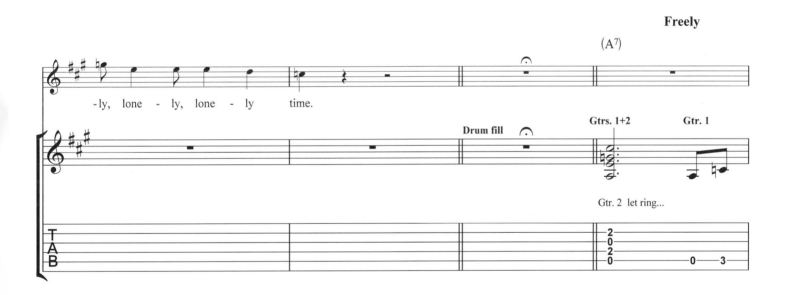

-ly, lone - ly, lone - ly time.

123456789

FULL INSTRUMENTAL PERFORMANCES (WITH GUITAR):

DISC 1:
1. Communication Breakdown
(Page/Plant/Jones/Bonham) Warner/Chappell North America Limited.

2. Dazed And Confused
(Page) Warner/Chappell North America Limited.

3. Whole Lotta Love
(Page/Plant/Jones/Bonham) Warner/Chappell North America Limited.

4. Heartbreaker
(Page/Plant/Jones/Bonham) Warner/Chappell North America Limited.

5. Immigrant Song
(Page/Plant) Warner/Chappell North America Limited.

6. Since I've Been Loving You
(Page/Plant/Jones) Warner/Chappell North America Limited.

7. Black Dog
(Page/Plant/Jones) Warner/Chappell North America Limited.

8. Rock And Roll
(Page/Plant/Jones/Bonham) Warner/Chappell North America Limited.

BACKING TRACKS ONLY (WITHOUT GUITAR):

DISC 2:
1. Communication Breakdown
2. Dazed And Confused
3. Whole Lotta Love
4. Heartbreaker
5. Immigrant Song
6. Since I've Been Loving You
7. Black Dog
8. Rock And Roll